Amazing Hairstyle Tricks

DISNEY FROZEN
AMAZING HAIRSTYLE TRICKS
— Inspired by Anna & Elsa

© 2015 Disney Enterprises, Inc.

Author: Theodora Mjoll Skuladottir Jack/Olafur Gunnar Gudlaugsson
Photographer: Gassi.is
Layout and design: Olafur Gunnar Gudlaugsson
Cover design: Olafur Gunnar Gudlaugsson
Editors: Tinna Proppe, tinna@eddausa.com and Olafur Gunnar Gudlaugsson
Printing: Printed in Canada

Distributed by Midpoint Book Sales & Distribution

ISBN: 978-1-94078-735-0

www.eddausa.com

Amazing Hairstyle Tricks

44 Great Ideas Inspired by Anna and Elsa

Contents

Let Your Imagination Guide You

Welcome to this nifty guide to using hair accessories and creating your own fantastic designs!

Our favorite sisters from Arendelle don't always have time to do their hair and are busy with having fun with their friends but when they take the time they use so many fun hair accessories such as ribbons, flowers and hairpins! In this book you can learn how to use their style as inspiration to make your very own hair accessories.

Let your creativity and imagination guide you and use the tips and methods in this great book to create new designs that you can call your own.

The only thing to keep in mind is to be careful when using the hot glue gun and let an adult supervise you along the way.

Basic Hair Care

Care for Your Hair

Have you ever wondered how to care for your hair
to make it beautiful like Anna and Elsa's?
What to do before, during and after shampooing?
Well here are a few good tips on how to care for your hair.
Be sure to let your mom or dad help you.

How to choose your shampoo

First, you need to define your hair type. Is it
fine and thin? Thick and rough? Or maybe dry
or oily or something else entirely. Only once
you've defined your hair type can you choose
your shampoo. Be sure to have an adult read the
label and ascertain that the type of shampoo is
appropriate for your hair.

How to wash your hair

It's recommended to wash your hair twice with
shampoo. The reason for this is that you get all
the excess oils out and the hair stays cleaner for a
longer time.

Step 1 Wet your hair completely. Put an
appropriate amount of shampoo in your palm and
rub your hands together.

Step 2 Rub the shampoo firmly into your scalp.
Remember to rub the top of the scalp and back very
well.

Step 3 Drag the froth created down the length of the hair. Do this a few times. Remember that the main thing is to rub and wash the scalp thoroughly, not the length of the hair.

Step 4 Rinse the hair thoroughly with warm water until the shampoo is completely gone.

Repeat steps 1 to 4 one more time - but this time with a lot less shampoo.

Conditioner

Be sure to choose a conditioner that is appropriate for your type of hair, just like the shampoo. Put the conditioner into the hair, right after rinsing the shampoo. Be sure to rub it at least 1 inch away from the scalp and down the length of the hair. Doing this prevents the scalp from becoming oily and your hair stays cleaner and fluffier for a longer time.

After washing

After washing, dry your hair with a towel. You have to be careful when you comb wet hair. When your hair is wet it is more elastic and therefore more prone to breakage. Use combs with widely-spaced teeth or soft brushes. See more tips on page 13.

Tip

After towel-drying your hair, try using custom made hair oils or leave-in-conditioners. They moisten and soften the hair and make it easier to comb and manage while wet and after it is dry. They also protect the hair from dryness and damage from heat or cold.

Keeping the Hair Healthy

It is necessary to cut your hair on a regular basis to keep it healthy and remove damaged or fried ends. Many think that the hair grows faster if it is cut, but that is not the case. The hair is not "alive" and therefore cutting has no effect on its rate of growth.

But a good and healthy diet can have a very positive effect on hair growth. Vitamins like B5 (Pantothenic acid), A, E, B and C are great (in moderate amounts). Zinc, protein, magnesium and iron are also beneficial.

Learning proper hairstyling can be a long and sometimes arduous process. So be sure to seek a professional hairstylist when you decide to cut your hair.

Brushes & Combs

There are many different brushes and combs!
How do we tell the difference?

It is easy to get confused with so many different types of combs and brushes and it's often difficult to choose the right type. Brushes with soft bristles are best because they don't tear tangled hair.

Method

The best way to comb your hair is to start at the ends and work your way up the length of the hair, always combing or brushing away from the scalp. If you start near the scalp and drag the brush down the length of the hair, it will most often get tangled in the middle. So, start at the ends and move gradually up to prevent unnecessary tangles.

Note

Wash the brushes regularly with shampoo or disinfectant. Natural oils from the hair, bacteria and other dirt tend to stick to the bristles and make your hair dirty sooner.

Hot Irons

Hot irons are a great asset to hairstyling. They have a wide variety of uses and can make the difference between a nice hairstyle and a fabulous one!

We often tend to choose hot irons based on how they look or how costly they are instead of looking at how they really treat our hair. Good irons are more expensive for various reasons, but mainly because they treat our hair better.

How to use

Only use a hot iron on dry hair. Wet or damp hair will not curl, so be sure to dry your hair thoroughly before using a hot iron.

Hot irons work best at a temperature of 320°f – 450°f. That is extremely hot if you think about it. The heat can easily damage your hair or make it dry and matte. To avoid this, be sure to use some heat protection on your hair before using a hot iron. Heat protection is a lotion you massage into the hair.

Most heat protection is applied to wet hair but some on dry, so read the instructions carefully before applying.

When you curl or straighten your hair, start dividing the hair into manageable parts. You then start curling or straightening at the base and back of the crown, moving further up the head until the desired effect is achieved.

Do's and Don'ts

We hope this hairstyle guide is helpful and that it sparks your creativity! Here are a few more helpful tricks. Enjoy and good luck!

Don't put bright bobby pins into dark hair and vice versa. There are so many colors available, so choose the pin that matches the hair the closest.

Avoid elastic bands with iron bindings. The iron can damage or tear the hair, especially with frequent use. It's possible to get elastics with no bindings or soft bindings that don't tear the hair.

Have a grown up help with curling or flattening the hair with a hot iron. The iron can get up to 450°f so caution is advised. Gloves are recommended.

Be sure to have a safe space before you turn on a hot iron. Put a coaster or something non-flamable under the iron and make sure nothing else is going to touch the iron. It is very hot and can melt other things if they are too close.

Wash the hair with running water, not bath water. Running water from a shower does a better job cleaning the hair and it stays clean for a longer time.

Know your hair before buying hair products. Is it curly, flat, short, long thin or thick? Be sure to choose the right product for the hair. It is so common to buy hair products that are heavily advertised or something that is recommended by a friend but can be damaging to your hair type.

Don't fiddle with your hair. Oils and all kinds of dirt can easily be transferred from your fingers and the hair gets dirty sooner.

Chlorine in swimming pools can dry out the hair and is particularly bad for people with blonde hair. It's better to use a bathing cap in a chlorinated pool and be sure to rinse the hair right after swimming.

Tame baby hairs along your hairline by grabbing them between your fingers and coaxing them in the same direction as the rest of your hair as you tend to it with the dryer.

Fantastic Tricks

Thick or Thin Hair

It can be difficult to know whether your hair is thick or thin and it can also vary greatly. One year we have thicker hair than the next year! Here are a few tips on how to add volume to thin hair and decrease the volume of thick hair!

1.

2.

3.

4.

How to Thicken Thin Hair

Here are a few options to thicken your hair.

Option 1
Lift up the roots of the hair with a soft brush while blow drying thoroughly.

Option 2
Apply volumizing hair products into dry hair and blow dry again.

Option 3
Put plastic hair rolls into damp hair and let it dry.

Option 4
Curl your hair with a hot iron or a non-heat method (see pages 24, 26, 76 and 78).

5a.

5b.

Option 5
Lift the hair with a flat iron

Divide the hair on the side and pin away the top half. Put the flat iron around a thin layer of hair, hold firmly and release.

Repeat the process with another thin layer from the top half.

Do not use the flat iron on the top layer at the end of the process.

The result is a great lifting that will endure until the next wash.

How to Thin out Thick Hair

The easiest way to make your hair appear thinner is to flatten it with a straightening iron. It's that simple! There are also many products available that add weight to your hair and smooth and straighten out frizzy or curly hair.

Teasing Your Hair

Teasing your hair may seem like a very complicated process, but here it is made simple. Teasing can be used in many different ways, for example it is great to tease the hair a little bit before creating Elsa's iconic braid. It will make the braid look thicker!

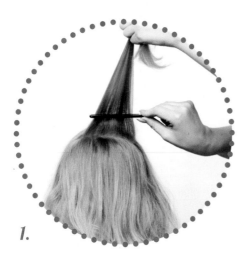

1.

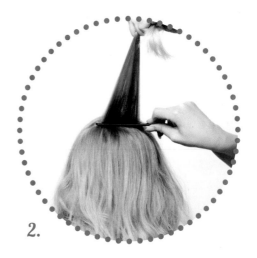

2.

Step 1

From the top of the head, take a lock of hair, no wider than the comb, and hold it firmly. Put the comb into the lock about 2 inches from the crown. Push the comb slowly but firmly down tight to the crown.

Take the comb out and move it a bit further up the lock. Again, push it firmly down the lock to the crown or until a sort of nest is formed. Repeat this method further up the lock as desired. When done, move the lock forward so it will not be in the way.

Step 2

Take another lock from behind the first and repeat step 1. Do this throughout the crown or as far as desired.

Step 3

Do the same with the sides, but be sure to make a distinctive divide between the sides and the top of the crown.

4.

Step 4

After having teased all the desired sections of hair, comb the hair while holding the comb at a 45º angle to the hair to prevent the teeth from pulling at the teased areas. This will hide the teased areas with a layer of neatly combed hair. The more you comb, the more you hide the tease.

No-Heat Curls 1

How did girls like Elsa and Anna curl their hair back in a time
before there was electricity for curling irons?
Here is one easy and fabulous way.

1.

2.

3.

4a.

Step 1

This process is best done before you go to sleep.
Lightly spray the hair with water before you begin but be sure to not overdo it. The hair should be lightly damp. Then place a long elastic around the hair.

Step 2

Take a hefty lock of hair near the face and wrap it once around the elastic band.

Step 3

Take another lock of hair and combine it with the former and wrap them once around the elastic band.

Step 4

Repeat this process all the way down to the back of the crown and then repeat on the other side of the head until all of your hair is wrapped neatly around the elastic band.

Step 5

After a good night's rest and with the hair dry, loosen the hair from the elastic band.

Step 6

Remove the elastic band, shake the hair thoroughly and brush it with a soft brush.

Now you have gorgeous no-heat curls!

4b.   5.   6.

25

No-Heat Curls 2

Here is another way to curl your hair using socks ... preferably clean ones!

1a.   1b.   1c.   1d.   1e.   1f.

2a.

2b.

2c.

3.

Step 1

Split the hair into three parts. Start at the top and roll the hair into the sock and tie a knot. It is best to have the hair a bit damp.

Step 2

Repeat with the other parts on the sides of the head. Leave overnight.

Step 3

Take out the socks in the morning and shake or comb the hair, as desired.

Hide the Elastic Band

You make a beautiful braid and have to use an elastic band to fasten it. But it doesn't match the color of your dress! Here is an easy way to make those pesky elastic bands disappear.

1.

2a.

Step 1
Take a small lock from the ponytail.

Step 2
Wrap the lock tightly around the elastic band.

2b.

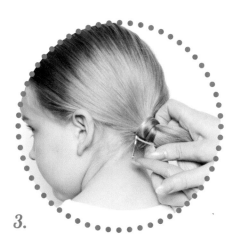

3.

Step 3

Pin down the end of the lock with a bobby pin.

Push the bobby pin under the elastic band until it is firmly in place.

There you go. No elastic band.

Using Bobby Pins

Here are some cool instructions to use bobby pins in an effective way at the top of the crown, on the sides, in hairstyles and everything in between.

The best way for a bobby pin to hold the hair together is to push it against the hair.

Step 1

Take a lock of hair with one hand and hold an open bobby pin with the other. Then slide the pin through the lock with both ends of the pin directed to the crown.

Step 2

Slide the bobby pin deep into the lock with your fingertips until it doesn't show anymore.

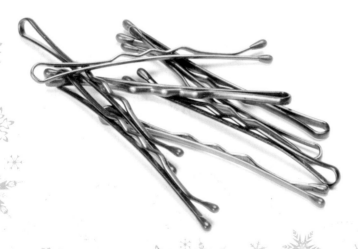

Step 3

If a lock is too thick or the desired area you want to pin down is too large, then use multiple bobby pins side by side with the same method listed above.

Hide Elastics with Ribbons

Those pesky elastics! Here's how we hide them with a beautiful bow made from a ribbon.

What you need

Elastic bands
Ribbon
Scissors

Ribbons

Elastic bands

1.

2a.

2b.

3.

Step 1
With the hair pulled back into a ponytail, thread a pre-cut ribbon through the elastic band.

Step 2
Wrap the ribbon once or twice around the elastic band and tie a knot.

Step 3
Make a bow from the remaining length of ribbon.

Step 4
Crop the ends of the bow as desired.

Accessorizing With a Scarf

Scarves can be so elegant and stylish. Here is one fantastic way to accessorize your hairstyle with a scarf.

What you need

A long scarf
Small elastic bands

1.

2.

Scarf

Step 1
Lay the scarf over the head and put it under the hair on one side.

Step 2
Twist the scarf to make a sort of rope.

Step 3
Use the twisted length of scarf and your own hair to make a braid.

Small elsatic bands

3a.

3b.

3c.

Step 4

Put a small elastic band at the end
to secure the braid.

Making Your Hairbrush Special

Beautifully decorated hairbrushes are often more expensive than the plain ones. Here is how you can make your own special hairbrush.

What you need

Hairbrush
Glue
Glitter dust
Paintbrush

Step 1
Apply glue on the whole backside of the brush with a paintbrush.

Step 2
Sprinkle the glitter dust evenly over the glue, covering the whole backside of the brush.

Step 3
Keep in a cool place to dry thoroughly.

Glue

Glitter dust

Brush

Unique Accessories

Decorate With Pearls

Accessories are something added to an existing item. They can be anything imaginable. In this case the hair was braided and it looks lovely on its own ... but we can always add accessories to it, and some pearls could be just the thing!

What you need
Plastic pearls
Hair pins
Glue gun

Before we begin, let's discuss the tools that are used in this book. When using any tool for the first time you should always proceed with caution. A glue gun, for example, can be a very safe, handy and useful tool, but it heats glue to a very high temperature. You should be extra careful with the glue gun and always have an adult present when using it.

Glue gun

Hair pins

Plastic pearls

Glue

40

Step 1

Decide how many pins you want to create and gather enough material for them. Take one pearl and put one small drop of glue on one side. Be careful not to use too much, and watch out for your fingers as the glue can be quite hot.

Step 2

Push the top end of a pin into the glued part of the pearl immediately, before the glue has cooled and hardened.

Step 3

Hold the pearl and the pin firmly together until the glue has dried. Create as many pearl accessories as you intend to use!

Step 4

Stick the pearl-pins into a beautiful hairdo.
It is always better to arrange the pearls into a nice pattern.

Decorate With Flowers

In Arendelle, where Anna and Elsa have lived all their lives, beautiful flowers can be found everywhere in the summertime. Here is a great and simple way to use flowers to create a fabulous hairstyle.

What you need

Silk flowers
Hair pins
Glue gun

For this decoration we recommend using silk flowers. Most convenience stores have them, but if you can't find any in your neighborhood, try using paper flowers or plastic. The end result will be great either way!

Glue gun

Hair pins

Glue

Silk flowers

Step 1

Silk flowers usually come with plastic stems attached to them. Cut away the stem and put one small drop of glue on the cut half of the flower. Be careful not to use too much, and remember that the glue is hot and can burn your fingers.

Step 2

Push the top end of a pin into the glued part of the flower before the glue has cooled and hardened.

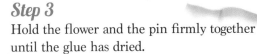

Step 3

Hold the flower and the pin firmly together until the glue has dried.

Step 4

Stick the flower-pin into a beautifull hairdo. Repeat as desired.

Create a Tiara

Have you ever wondered how to make a tiara?
Here is one design inspired by Elsa's coronation tiara.

The pattern for this tiara is easily replicated. Just remember that it does not need to be perfect. The main thing is to have fun while creating something beautiful.

Step 1
Fold the silver paper once in half. Draw the outlines of the tiara on the folded side. You can copy the picture below or use your imagination.

What you need

Silver glitter paper
Blue glitter paper
Headband
An ornament
Scissors
Pencil

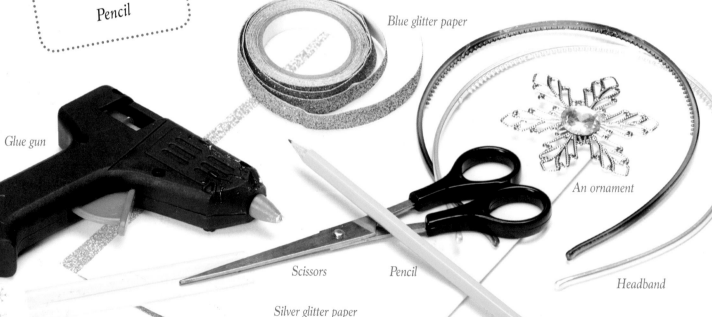

Blue glitter paper

An ornament

Glue gun

Scissors   Pencil

Headband

Silver glitter paper

Step 2
Cut out the tiara following the outlines. Note that if the paper is not stiff enough, then use a double layer and glue them together.

Step 3
Glue the cut-out onto the center of the headband.

Step 4
Paste an ornament on the tiara with the glue gun.

Step 5
Cut out a ribbon of the blue paper, preferably a bit wider than the headband. Glue the ribbon of blue paper around the headband with the glue gun.

Elsa's Ribbon Decoration

When accessorizing with ribbons you can experiment
with lots of colors and different ornaments.
Here is a version inspired by Elsa's style.

What you need

Different
colored ribbons
of different width
Decorative hair pin
Scissors

For this hair accessory, we
recommend using decorative hair
pins. They are available in any store
carrying hair accessories.

Ribbons

*Decorative
hair pins*

Step 1

Cut one wide ribbon and two narrow ones to your desired length

Step 2

Tie them tightly to the top of the hair pin.

Step 3

Do this for each ribbon, one at a time, until all ribbons are tied to the top of the hair pin.

Step 4

Pin the ribbon decoration into your beautiful hairdo.

Anna's Ribbon Decoration

Here is another way to use ribbons when decorating your hairdo.
This is inspired by Anna's colors and her great use of ribbons!

What you need

Colored ribbons
Decorative hair clip
Scissors
Glue gun

Decorative hair clips

Ribbons

Glue gun

Step 1
Cut the ribbons into equal lengths.

Step 2
Glue together on one end with the glue gun. Trim the edges as shown in the inserted picture to the left.

Step 3
Use the glue gun to secure the ribbons behind the decorative feature of the hair clip. Let everything cool completely before continuing.

Step 4
Stick the ribbon decoration into a beautiful bun or hairdo.

Snowball Headband

Headbands never go out of style. They can be so practical and also a lot of fun. Especially when you create a snowball headband!

What you need

A long elastic band
Wool thread
Scissors
Glue

Elastic band

Glue

Wool thread

Step 1

Wrap the wool thread firmly arround two fingers.

Step 2

Remove the thread bundle from the fingers and tie a shorter length of thread around the bundle.

Step 3

Clip the two sides of the bundle creating snowballs. Repeat as desired.

Step 4

Glue the little snowballs onto the elastic band.

Decorate Hair Combs 1

Hair combs are very useful accessories with many applications...
even more so if you decorate them!

What you need

Ribbon
Hair comb
Glue gun
Plastic pearls

Step 1

Wrap the end of the comb with a long ribbon.
It is best to glue the ribbon to the comb at the
beginning and at the end.

Step 2

Take a pearl and put one small
drop of glue on one side of it.

Hair comb

Ribbon

Glue gun

Plastic pearls

Step 3
Press the glued end of the pearl
onto the wrapped end of the comb.

Step 4
Hold the pearl tightly in place until the glue
has dried. Repeat until the length of the comb
has been lined with pearls. Let cool.

Step 5
Place the comb into a lovely hairdo.

Decorate Hair Combs 2

This hair comb is created to match the frosty look of Elsa in her ice palace! It looks elaborate but is very easy to make!

What you need

Ribbon
Hair comb
Gem stones
Glue gun

To get the icy look of the comb it is optional to glue tinfoil on the comb and then trim it a bit with scissors.

Glue gun

Hair comb

Ribbon

Gem stones

Step 1

Cut equal lengths of ribbon and tie them around the base of the comb at even intervals.

Step 2

Secure the gems to the comb using your hot glue gun and the same method described on pages 52-53. To get an icier look, glue tinfoil to the base of the comb and paste the pearls on top of it!

Step 3

Place the comb into a lovely hairdo.

The Flower Crown

Remember when we mentioned that Arendelle is filled with flowers in the summertime? Well, what better way to accessorize than with a whole crown of blossoms?

What you need

Flower wire
Silk flowers
Scissors
Glue gun

Step 1

Make a circle from the flower wire that fits the head of the intended wearer. Use 3 or 4 strands of wire, with the ends tied together, for strength and thickness.

Step 2

Silk flowers usually come with plastic stems attached. Cut away the stem and put one small drop of glue on the cut half of the flower.

Step 3

Press the flower to the wire until the glue is dry. Continue around the entire circle. Use your imagination in creating a dynamic flower crown. For variation, try putting some leaves behind the flowers!

Glue gun

Silk flowers

Flower wire

Decorating the Elastic Bands

It's not that we don't like elastic bands. It's just that they are so... plain.
Try this fun way to make your elastic bands more frosty or flowery!

The possibilities of this particular accessory are limited only by your imagination! Choose any decoration and it will turn any plain elastic band into a great accessory for your lovely hair.

Plastic flowers

Silk flowers

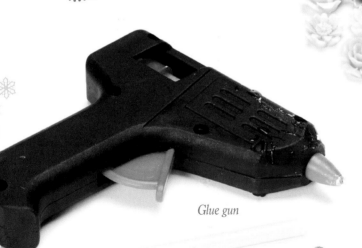

Glue gun

Elastic bands

Pearls and gems

Step 1
Put a drop of glue onto any decoration.

Step 2
Push the elastic band and the decoration firmly together and hold steadily until the glue has dried. Let cool.

Step 3
Fasten the beautiful elastic band on a braid, pigtails, ponytail or any other hairstyle that requires an elastic band.

A Bow Decoration

Elegant and simple to make, the bow is always a good way to go.

What you need

Ribbon
Hair pin
Decoration
Glue gun
Thread

Step 1

Fold a ribbon together as shown in the picture. Trim the ends into a V shape.

Step 2

Use the thread to tie the folded ribbon securely in its center.

Ribbon

Glue gun

Plastic flowers

Hair pins

Scissors

Step 3
Tie a hair pin to the ribbon
using thread.

Step 4
Glue a decoration on the side
facing out with a glue gun.

Step 5
Add the bow to your fabulous
hairstyle!

Headband With a Flower Twist

Flowers come in all shapes and sizes.
This elegant decoration is both simple and useful.

What you need

Headband
Silk flowers,
with wire stems

Silk flowers

Step 1
Secure the flowers to the headband by wrapping and twisting the wire stems around the band.

Step 2
Put the floral headband onto a head of lovely curled hair or other elegant hairstyle.

Headband

Snowflake Headband

It isn't always flowers and summertime in Arendelle. Here is a beautiful headband that is inspired by Elsa and her unique talent!

What you need

A strip of snowflake trim

Long elastic band

Glue gun

Stapler

Gem stones

Step 1

Cut a length of snowflake trim 5 inches shorter than the circumference of the wearer's head. Ready-made snowflake trims are mostly available at any arts and crafts store. If you want to create your own you can use the template provided on the nex page. Choose a fabric you wish to use and cut it in the length and width of the desired headband. Fold the fabric lengthwise like an accordion. Place the template on top of the folded fabric and cut along it. Be careful only to cut on the top and bottom and not on the folded sides.

Step 2

Staple an elastic band to the ends of the snowflake trim, keeping the size so that the headband will fit tightly around the head.

Step 3

Decorate as desired with gem stones.

Glue gun

Stapler

Elastic band

Snowflake trim

A Big Flower Headband

When you want to go all out and accessories with beautiful big flowers, this is the headband for you.

What you need

Soft felt
Elastic band
Glue gun
Stapler
Silk flowers
Scissors

Stapler

Silk flowers

Soft felt

Glue gun

Elastic band

Scissors

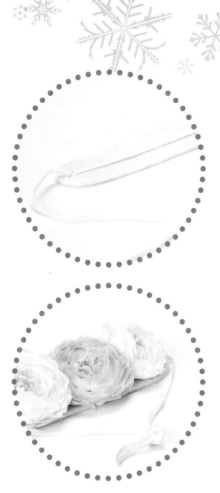

Step 1

Cut the felt into an elongated shape. Cut a length of elastic band to the size of the wearer's head and staple it to the felt.

Step 2

Turn the felt over and glue silk flowers to it in any arrangement.Use your imagination. Hold the flowers firmly to the felt until the glue has dried.

Step 3

Add the flower headband to an elegant hairstyle.

Marvelous Hairstyles

Elsa's Icy Braid

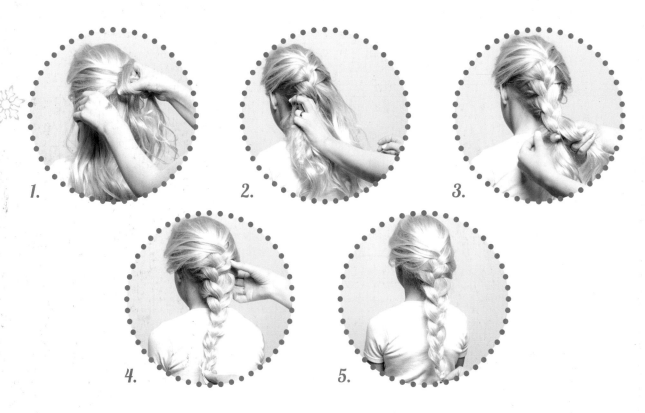

1.

2.

3.

4.

5.

Step 1
Take three locks of hair along the hairline in the front and move the lock of hair on the right over the lock in the middle.

Step 2
Now take the lock of hair on the left and move it over the one that is in the middle and take the lock of hair on the right and add a small lock of hair laying next to it, to the lock.

Step 3
Move the lock of hair on the right along with the added hair over the lock of hair in the middle. Repeat this process to the lock of hair on the left and all the way down until all the hair on the head has been added to the braid.

Step 4
Pull the ends of the braid. It works well to hold onto the end of the braid with one hand while pulling its ends with the other hand.

Step 5
Put a small elastic band at the end.

Anna's Ponytail

As you know Anna is busy with many different things and she loves walking around Arendelle and meeting new people as well as having fun with her friends. She doesn't always have time to put her hair up in a beautiful hairdo. Here is a great hairstyle for when you are short on time!

1.

2.

2a.

2b.

Step 1
Begin with dividing the hair into two equal parts at the back of the crown.

Step 2
Tie a knot at the nape of the neck. Be sure to have it tight but not overly so.

Step 3
Put an elastic band up against the knot to hold it in place.

Tip
The smaller the elastic band the better. If you want the elastic to disappear then use the hairstyle trick on page 28.

2c.

3a.

3b.

Super Long Ponytail

All girls love ponytails. The longer the better.
But sometimes our hair just isn't long enough.

Step 1
Separate a large amount of hair from the sides and top of the crown from the hair on the back of the head (see picture).

Step 2
Make ponytails from both parts using elastic bands.

Step 3
Lay both tails down and stretch the top tail to both sides so it hides the lower tail.

Step 4
Hide the elastic band of your ponytail using the method on page 28.

That's how easy it is!

Curling with an Iron 1

Now you can try one of two ways to curl your hair with a hot iron. Follow these steps carefully and always remember to only use a hot iron on dry hair.

1.

2.

2b.

3a.

3b.

4.

What you need is a hot curling iron and a hair clip.

Step 1
Start below at the base of the crown.

Step 2
Keep the curling iron level under a lock of hair and wrap it tightly around the iron. Repeat this process.

Step3
Use the same method going slowly up to the top of the crown, keeping the iron horizontal.

Step 4
Shake and brush the hair after it has cooled down.

Curling with an Iron 2

Here is the second way to curl your hair with a hot iron with a
slightly different method.

1a.

2a.

2b.

2c.

3.

4.

What you need is a hot
curling iron and a hair clip.

Step 1
Start below at the base of the
crown.

Step 2
Turn the curling iron vertical
by a lock of hair and wrap
it tightly around the iron.
Repeat the process.

Step3
Use the same method going
slowly up to the top of the
crown, keeping the iron
vertical.
Turn the iron away from
both sides of the face.

Step 5
Shake and brush the hair
after it has cooled down.

The Topsy Tail™

The Topsy-Tail™ is an ingenious, easy-to-use hair tool. Invented in 1991, this great tool can make all the difference for that great hairstyle. What it does is it creates a very nice loop in the hair that can be used for various styling tricks.

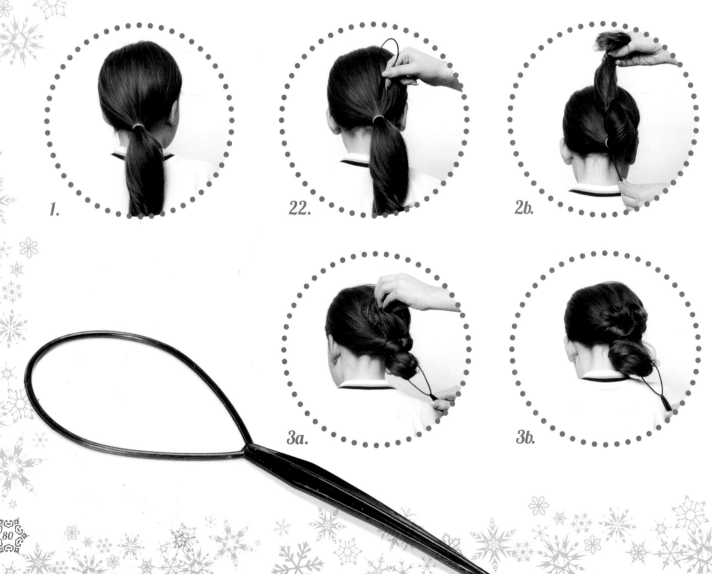

1.

22.

2b.

3a.

3b.

4.

Step 1
Gather all your hair to create a ponytail.

Step 2
Stick the Topsy Tail™ into the hair behind the elastic band and pull the ponytail through its loop.

Step 3
Drag the Topsy Tail™ through the hair or until it comes loose from the hair.

Step 4
Arrange the tail as desired.

Anna's Braids

Here is the way to make Anna's beautiful braids.

Step 1
Divide the hair in two sections. Make a shallow side part at the front. If you have a light hair lock or a ribbon, by all means fasten it in the hair on one side.

Step 2
Bring all the hair on one side over the ear and divide it into three parts. Braid the hair, with the lock closest to the face added first into the braid.

Step 3
Put a small elastic band on the end.

Step 4
Take a small lock from below the elastic band and wrap it around it.

Step 5
Pin the end down by placing a bobby pin behind the braid and pressing it. You can also use a small rubber band, which holds longer.

The Bun Maker

The bun maker is another ingenious hair tool. Here is an easy way to work with the bun maker. This is a great tool to create a nice up-do like Anna's hairstyle for the coronation.

1 and 2.

3a.

3b.

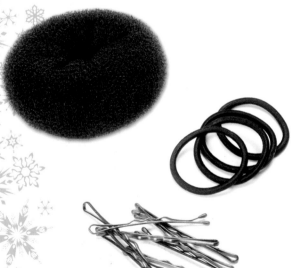

What you need is a bun maker, elastic bands and bobby pins.

Step 1
Create a ponytail and put the bun maker around the tail.

Step 2
Pin the bun maker down in 3-4 places with bobby pins. Hook one end into the bun maker and the other into the hair. Push into the elastic band.

Step 3
Spread the tail evenly over the bun and put an elastic over it.

Step 4
Divide the rest of the tail in two and wrap around the bun.

Step 5
Pin the ends down by hooking one end to the tail and the other into the root of the hair. Push the pin into the elastic band.

3c.

4a.

4b.

A Twisted Bun

There are many different ways to make a bun.
Here we show you how in only 5 minutes!
The style is inspired by Elsa's coronation hairstyle!

1.

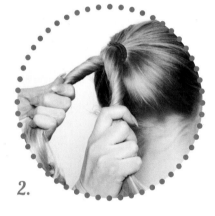

2.

3.

4a.

Step 1
Create a ponytail.

Step 2
Divide the tail into two parts and twist the locks in the same direction.

Step 3
Create a braid but in the opposite direction that you twisted the hair earlier.

Step 4
Continue down the length of the hair and fasten with an elastic band in the end.

Step 5
Wrap the braid around the elastic band and finally use bobby pins to strap it down.

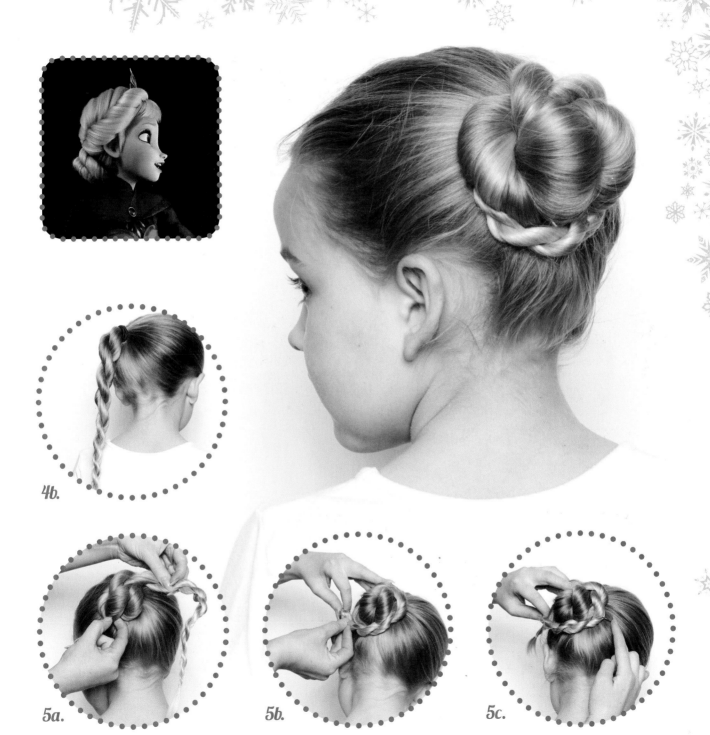

4b.

5a.

5b.

5c.

Anna's Hairdo

Learn how to make Anna's coronation hairstyle!

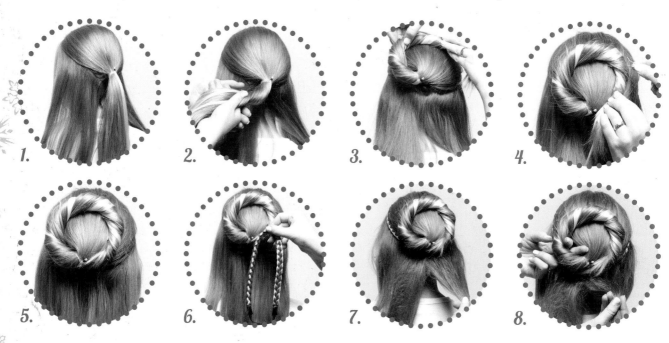

1.   2.   3.   4.

5.   6.   7.   8.

Step 1 Pull aside hair by the hairline on either side and put the middle section in a low ponytail. Tie a ribbon around the ponytail.

Step 2 Start twisting the hair from the ponytail tightly.

Step 3 Twist the ponytail, up along the head in a circle.

Step 4 Pin the bun tightly down around the circle.

Step 5 Try to make the twist as even as possible throughout the circle.

Step 6 Put a braided hairband around the hair. If the child has very thick hair, take a lock from underneath the twist, braid it and wrap it around the hair instead of the hairband.

Step 7 Lightly backcomb the loose hair and divide it in two.

Step 8 Take hold of the left section and put two fingers under the twist on the right side.

Step 9 Pull the hair through, underneath the twist.

Step 10 Do the same thing on the other side.

Step 11 Press the ends of the hair into the bun that has formed at the back, and pin the hair down.
It's best to hook the pin into the bulge and the root of the hair, then push it in and down into the hairdo. Decorate the middle of the hairdo with hair accessories à la Anna.

9.

10.

11.

Using Elastic Bands 1

Using elastic bands to create intricate designs in your hair may seem complicated at first, but these instructions will help you turn your hair into a work of art with simple elastic bands.

What you need

Small elastic bands

Step 1

For extra fun, use different colored elastic bands. Take four medium sized locks of hair from the forehead on each side of the head.

Step 2

Put an elastic band around the first lock. Moving down the hair, secure the first lock to the second with another elastic band. Repeat this process, securing the third lock to the first two with another elastic band. Secure the fourth lock to the bunch with another elastic band.

Small elsatic bands

Step 3

Repeat Step 2 on the other side of the head.

Step 4

Combine the two locks at the back of the head with the final elastic band.

Using Elastic Bands 2

And now you are ready to become a master of elastic art.

Small elsatic bands

Step 1

Take a medium sized lock of hair from the centre of the head, near the forehead. Secure this lock into a small ponytail using an elastic band.

Step 2

Take another lock from near the forehead, to the right of the first. Secure it with an elastic band.

Step 3

Divide each of the small ponytails you've just made in two and combine the halves closest to one another with another elastic band. Repeat this process down the back of the hair, creating a lattice pattern.

Step 4

Repeat this process on the other side of the head.

Index